Une vague de rêves
A Wave of Dreams

D1512648

This publication is dedicated to John Rety
1930-2010

A WAVE OF DREAMS
by Louis Aragon 1924

translated by Susan de Muth 2010

Thin Man Press

Indeed Productions

Une Vague de Rêves first published 1924
© Editions Seghers

English translation copyright © Susan de Muth 2006 revised 2010

Introduction copyright © Dawn Adès, 2006

CD copyright © Indeed Productions

This translation first published online in *Papers of Surrealism* 2006.

Frst print edition English translation, this publication and design

© Thin Man Press (part of Indeed Productions) 2010

ISBN: 978-0-9562473-1-5

Contents

Introduction
by Professor Dawn Adès

In 1924 the surrealist movement emerged from the period of trances and dreams. It was not the only one to lay claim to this word coined by Apollinaire, but it quickly saw off its rivals such as Ivan Goll, whose single issue review *Surréalisme*, which appeared in October 1924, attempted in vain to wrest 'surrealism' back from those who were making of it a new way of life, and to fix it as a form of modernist expression rooted in film. 'Surrealism' was a term already in use during the period of trances, whose power as a word was firmly harnessed by Breton in his description of those trance sessions in 'Entry of the Mediums' (*Littérature* November 1922): 'by it we have agreed to designate a certain psychic automatism which corresponds quite closely to the dream state...'

It is true, as Aragon implies in his later comment about *Une Vague de rêves*, quoted below, that his text lays more importance on these experiences than does Breton's *Surrealist Manifesto*. The latter, laying out a possible future for a practice of automatism that will explore the hidden realm of the unconscious, underplays the experiments in self-hypnosis in favour of the earlier experiments in automatic writing undertaken, Breton claims, under the influence of Freud. Aragon's text is a vital account of the experience of the *mouvement flou* and the embrace of chance and the unknown, but he does not place it under the signboard of Freud. Dreams loosen the sense of self and usher in chance and the unexpected.

October 1924 saw not only the publication of Aragon's *Une Vague de rêves* and Breton's *Surrealist Manifesto* and but also the opening of the Bureau of Surrealist Research at 15 rue de Grenelle where the public were invited to enter and tell their dreams. Memorable descriptions in Aragon's text of this 'romantic lodgings for unclassifiable ideas and revolutions in progress' suggest that it might have been contemporaneous with, rather than anterior to, this crucial consolidation of collective activity.

The Historical Context

by Susan de Muth

In published interviews Aragon was emphatic that *Une Vague de rêves* - submitted to the journal *Commerce* in June 1924 (but published in the October) - preceded André Breton's *Surrealist Manifesto* which was written in the summer of 1924.

Aragon's poem-essay was the first work, then, to identify, evaluate and document the dazzling new surrealist movement as it emerged from the still smouldering embers of Dada.

Une Vague de rêves is a lyrical and vivid account of the lifestyle, intellectual processes and enthusiastic experimentations of the early surrealists, mostly young men in their twenties.

Later attempts to underplay Aragon's role in the history of surrealism - largely a result of political differences within the group - meant that the significance of *Une Vague de rêves* (which Aragon describes as his 'testament') was long overlooked.

Whilst Aragon acknowledged the importance of Breton's *Surrealist Manifesto* in its own right, he nevertheless insisted (interviewed by his biographer,

Dominique Arban) that, 'The words surreality and surrealism are used and widely defined in my text as if they were indeed part of a manifesto for the surrealist movement which came into being just a few months later.'

Why droops my Celia? Thou hast in place of a base husband found A worthy lover; use thy fortune well, With secrecy and pleasure. See, behold What thou art queen of; [He shows her the treasure] not in expectation, As I feed others, but possessed and crowned. See, here, a rope of pearl, and each more orient Than that the brave Egyptian queen caroused; Dissolve and drink 'em. See, a carbuncle May put out both the eyes of St Mark; A diamond would have bought Lollia Paulina When she came in like star-light, hid with jewels That were the spoils of provinces; take these, And wear, and lose 'em; yet remains an earring To purchase them again, and this whole state. A gem but worth a private patrimony Is nothing; we will eat such a meal. The heads of parrots, tongues of nightingales, The brains of peacocks, and of ostriches Shall be our food, and, could we get the phoenix, Though nature lost her kind, she were our dish.

Ben Jonson *Volpone*

S ometimes, quite suddenly, I lose the whole thread of my life: sitting in some corner of the universe, by a smoky dark café, polished bits of metal set out before me, tall, mild-mannered women ebbing and flowing around me, I start to wonder what path of madness brought me here, washed up beneath this arch that is really the bridge they have named sky.

This is the moment of oblivion, the moment when vast fissures in the Palace of the World widen into daylight: I would give up the rest of my life - a paltry sum - if only it could endure. For then the mind detaches a little from the human machine and I am no longer my senses' bicycle, a grindstone honing memories and encounters. And then I grasp chance within me, I grasp all of a sudden how I surpass myself: I *am* chance, and having formed this proposition I laugh at the thought of all human activity.

This would certainly be a glorious moment to die; this is the moment, surely, when the clear-sighted ones who simply decide to leave one day do kill themselves. It is at this point, in any case, that thought begins; thought quite unlike the harmless looking-glass game many are so good at. Anyone who has experienced this vertigo even once would find it impossible to endorse the mechanistic ideas that nearly all man's present endeavours - and his entire peace of mind - can be reduced to.

Now the ill-considered axiom at the bottom of what seemed to be the purest thought-process is clear to see: clinging to a forgotten system, no longer scrutinized, left unchallenged like a rut in the mind. This is why philosophers talk in proverbs and feel they have to prove everything. They shackle their own imaginations with foreign rings, robbed in famous graves. By observing Truth in facets, they believe in only partial truths.

*

I lived in the shadow of a great white building adorned with flags and uproar. This castle was Society and I was not allowed to escape; those who climbed its steps created a terrible storm of dust on the threshold. Our country, honour, religion, goodness... it was hard to distinguish the innumerable words they hurled wildly into the echoes. Yet I gradually made out the beliefs they held most dear. These boiled down to very little. 'The inclination of every being to persist in its being' is one of their favourite expressions, though they rather disparage hedonism; they use the pejorative phrase 'marred by Finalism' to condemn anything and everything; and then there is this phrase which they particularly like and use to usher in the paragraphs of their intellectual lives: 'Let us draw aside the veil of words for a moment'. Little do they suspect that such processes lead them only to hypotheses, and *a posteriori* hypotheses at that. Their minds are monstrous hybrids, born of the grotesque conjugation of oyster and buzzard. But the hunchbacks of Thought need not fear that superstitious passers-by might brush against their deformity for good luck. They are the Kings of the World and the gaolers of the dungeon whence I hear their jovial songs and the sound of the keys they are jangling.

Every now and then a visitor would concern himself with how I was occupying my time in what was described (without irony) as my self-imposed seclusion. And if he fleetingly engaged with the strangeness of my existence, not knowing whether it was me he should doubt or himself, his eyes would swiftly glaze over with incredulity at everything I said. How could he believe that I am not in search of happiness? That thought exists only in words? Sometimes such a visitor, influenced by fashion, would declare himself for Idealism but all I could see was yet another shame-faced realist, like so many well-meaning men these days, subsisting on a compromise between Kant and Comte. By abandoning the commonplace notion of reality for the concept of reality within they believe they have made a great leap forward - but their idol, the Noumenon, has been exposed as a very mediocre piece of plaster. Nothing can make people like this understand the true nature of 'reality', that it is just an experience like any other, that the essence of things is not at all linked to their reality, that there are other experiences that the mind can embrace which are equally fundamental such as chance, illusion, the fantastic, dreams. These different types of experience are brought together and reconciled in one genre, Surreality.

*

The complicated provenance of ideas is quite awe-inspiring. The concept of Surreality could only emerge from a human consciousness already well acquainted with extraordinary schools of thought and the accumulated events of centuries.

Where then does it choose to spring up? It is 1919: André Breton is engaged in some very specific deliberations, resolving a particular poetic problem; at the point where the fundamental ethics of this problem are just becoming clear, and while applying himself to understanding the mechanism of the dream, he rediscovers on the threshold of sleep the threshold and nature of inspiration. When he makes this discovery - of great significance in its own right - he does not immediately realize its deeper implications, and neither does Philippe Soupault who participates with him in the first surrealist experiments.

What most impresses them is an Energy, a sense of no longer being themselves, an incomparable feeling of well-being, a liberation of the mind, an unprecedented ability to produce images and the supernatural tone of their writings. In all that now originates from them - and they have no sense of authorship in these creations - they recognise the matchlessness of certain books, of certain words which still exhilarate them.

They suddenly perceive a great poetic unity which runs from the prophetic works of all peoples to *Les Illuminations* and *Les Chants de Maldoror*. Between the lines they read the unfinished testimonies of people who once followed the System: in the flashlight of their discovery *Une Saison en enfer* sheds its mysteries, the Bible and other confessions of Man put aside their masks of images. But this is just before Dada, and what they deduce above all from their discoveries is the fallacy of 'genius'; their indignation mounts as they see how they've been duped by this illusion, by this fraud which suggests that literature is the result of a certain method, conceals that method, and then conceals the fact that this method is actually within everybody's reach.

Knowing they can expose it any time they wish, the first few surrealist pioneers allow this literary swindle to go unchallenged, wholly immersed in their first encounters with the enchanting depths. Initially they carry on in all tranquillity, for the world simply laughs at their songs.

What will suddenly alert them to the abyss beside which they have set up camp, what opens their eyes to the field of comets they've been tilling unawares, is the unforeseen impact of surrealism on their lives. They'd thrown themselves into it as if it were the sea, and now, just like a treacherous sea, surrealism threatens to sweep them out to the open ocean where the sharks of madness cruise.

*

I have often thought about the man who first came up with the idea of recording the vibrations of the voice: he put little sound-sensitive plates, carbon and copper wires all together into a machine and then actually did hear the unmistakable sound of the human voice. In the same way the first surrealists forced themselves into states of utter exhaustion through excesses viewed as mere games, and they saw the Marvellous arise before them, overwhelming hallucinations more usually produced by ecstatic religious states or narcotic drugs.

At that time we used to meet in the evenings like hunters, comparing what we'd bagged that day, the tally of beasts we'd invented, the fantastic plants, the images we'd shot down. In the grip of a tremendous momentum, we spent more and more time on the practices which led us into our strange inner lands. We delighted in observing the curve of our own exhaustion, and the derangement which followed. For then the Marvellous would appear.

At first each one of us thought himself subject to some peculiar mental disorder and struggled against it. Then it revealed its true nature. It was as if the mind, having reached a turning point in the subconscious, lost all control over where it was drifting.

Images which existed in the mind took on physical forms, became tangible reality. Once we were in touch with them they expressed themselves in a perceptible form, taking on the characteristics of visual, auditory and tactile hallucinations. We experienced the full force of these images. We could no longer control them. We had become *their* domain, a setting for them. In bed, at the moment of falling asleep, in the street with eyes wide open, with the full apparatus of dread, we held out our hands to phantoms.

Rest, abstention from surrealism made these phenomena disappear, gave us space to comprehend how close they were to the phenomena induced by chemical preparations, and at first we suspended our experiments through fear, but they gradually reclaimed their rights over our curiosity.

The nature of the troubled mental states brought on by surrealism, by physical fatigue, by narcotics, and the way these resembled dreams and mystical visions together with the semiology of mental illness led us to evolve this proposition which, alone, can explain and link all these factors: the existence of *a mental substance*.

The similarity between hallucinations and sensations compelled us to think of this mental substance as being different to thought, with thought itself, in all its perceptible manifestations, being only one particular example of it. The way we experienced it was through its concrete power, through its power to become concrete. We saw that it could pass from one state into another, and that these transmutations evidenced its existence as well as its nature.

We would see a written image, for example, which initially emerged at random, as if by chance, reach out to our senses, divest itself of its verbal element and take on the substance of phenomena we had only previously experienced in our imaginations, never knowing it was possible to coax them out and into a tangible form.

We now felt that every mental and physical experience was a direct result of our participation in this paradoxical exercise. Then, imagining the opposite of what we were experiencing, we reduced each sensation, each thought we wished to analyse, to a single word. *Absolute nominalism* was dazzlingly exemplified in surrealism and it gradually dawned on us that the mental substance described above was, in fact, vocabulary itself. *There is no thought outside words*: the whole surrealist experience evidences this proposition, nothing new in itself perhaps, yet greeted, nowadays, with more scepticism than all the vague opinions (constantly contradicted by facts) of realists who are swept along to the Pantheon one fine rainy evening.

We have seen then what the Surreal is about. But to really understand the concept we have to extend it; view it perhaps like the horizon which continually flees before the walker, for like the horizon this concept exists between the mind and what it knows it will never reach. Having weighed up its experience of the Real - in which it indiscriminately mixes everything that exists - the mind naturally juxtaposes what it knows of the Unreal. Only when the mind has gone beyond these two notions can it begin to envisage a wider experience, one where these other two experiences co-exist, and that is the Surreal.

Surreality, the state where these concepts are fused by the mind, is the shared horizon of religion, magic, poetry, dreaming, madness, intoxication and this fluttering honeysuckle, puny little life, that you believe capable of colonizing the heavens for us.

Clouds disperse on the smallest breath and the same wind brings them back. An idea too has its golden fringes. The sun plays a little with the phantoms. They dance well without ballet shoes and that broken chain at their ankles sets the price of their steps.

Oh phantoms with mutable eyes, children of the shadows, wait for me, I'm nearly there and you turn away. Do not go beyond the acacia blossom, the guard of honour, the tribune, here I am: and yet you turn down other hawthorned byways with your scarves woven from reflections and dominoes of perpetual abstraction.

How to follow an idea? Its paths are full of farandoles. Masks appear on balconies. The whole of life solicits us as we pass with our wives on our arms, offering us violets: everyone's problems in posies. My dear, another girl with something to sell, and over there, another kiss.

Dada was a moral trial and a phantom in its way. We lived out a haunted existence where the mind was not allowed to engage with concepts. A vague sentimental thread of the surreal ran through our intentions, like a foretaste of the abyss, anonymous as yet and faceless. One fine day the spectre tore himself free with his skeleton hands and made for the heights.

A prolonged period of stupefaction followed this parting of the clouds. The number of surrealists had grown. Young people intent on intoxication, derangement, frustration, who didn't miss the conflagrations of noise and demonstrations they'd left behind, still smouldering and certainly most beguiling. They instantly gave themselves up to vice, they hurled themselves into it.

The surrealist idea needed something - a circumstance like a ring on the finger of a woman just met, like a drawing on the wall of a waiting room - to take a new twist towards the unexpected. And this came about beside the sea when René Crevel met a lady who taught him how to get into an extraordinary hypnotic trance which was something like sleepwalking. In this condition he would utter the most beautiful, prolonged speeches. An outbreak of trances swamped the surrealists. By following an invented protocol - with varying degrees of precision - many of them discovered that they too had this ability.

Towards the end of 1922 - have you noticed how great flashes of inspiration often occur at this time of year? - there are seven or eight of them who live only for these moments of oblivion, when they talk with the lights out, without consciousness, like drowning men in the open air. These moments multiply by the day. They want to spend more and more time in oblivion. When told what they have uttered they are intoxicated by their own words.

They fall into trances everywhere. All they have to do now is perform the opening ritual. Robert Desnos has only to close his eyes in a café and, regardless of the sound of voices, the bright light, being jostled by passers-by, he starts to speak; amid the beer glasses and saucers the whole Ocean collapses with its prophetic din and vapours decorated with long oriflammes. Those who consult this prodigious man of trances have only gently to prompt him for outpourings of prophecy, the voice of magic, revelation and Revolution, the voice of the fanatic and the apostle to burst forth. Under other circumstances, even if he entered this delirium only rarely, Desnos would become the leader of a religion, the founder of a city, the tribune of a people in revolt. He speaks, he draws, he writes.

Coincidences start to characterize the outpourings of the sleepers. The era of collective hallucinations is born together with this question: are they really, after all, hallu-cinations? Those who submit themselves to these inces-sant experiments endure a constant state of appalling agitation, become increasingly manic. They grow thin.

Their trances last longer and longer. They no longer wish to be brought out of them. They go into trances to meet one another and converse like people in a far away world where everyone is blind; they quarrel and sometimes knives have to be snatched from their hands.

The very evident physical ravages suffered by the subjects of this extraordinary experiment, as well as frequent difficulties in wrenching them from a cataleptic death-like state, will soon force them to give in to the entreaties of the onlookers leaning on the parapet of wakefulness, and suspend the activities which neither laughter nor misgivings have hitherto affected.

And so the spirit of criticism reclaims its rights. People question whether or not they were really in a trance at all. Deep down some deny the whole adventure. The idea of simulation is tossed back into play. Personally I could never really get to grips with this suggestion. Is simulating something any different to thinking it? And once something has been thought, it exists. Nothing will change my mind on that. Besides, how can the inspired nature of the spoken dreams that unfolded before me be explained if they were simulated?

The whole spectacle had made such an impact that delirious explanations were called for: the hereafter, re-incarnation, the Marvellous. Such interpretations were greeted with mocking laughter and incredulity. In fact they were nearer the mark than was commonly supposed. A combination of chance events had made us the eager witnesses of phenomena which were essentially no different to all the supernatural facts that humble human reason throws into the future's basket of oblivion along with other equations it can't work out.

What is not in doubt is that this is part of surrealism's apparatus, where faith in the trance - in relation to the spoken word - corresponds to speed in written surrealism. And like speed, faith in the trance (and the dramas that accompany it) removes the impediment of self-censorship which so restrains the mind.

Freedom, that wonderful word, at last has a meaning: Liberty begins where the Marvellous is born. Now one can envisage collective surrealisms, surrealism convincing whole nations of miracles and military victo-ries and what actually happened at the Marriage at Cana and the battle of Valmy. At the foot of this magical

windmill it is true, and this alone is true, that the peasants'
water was changed into wine and blood and all the while
the hills were singing. Oh disbelieving madmen, you too
have bowed your heads before armed words as they
raised a large patch of the sky.

An idea once formed does not limit itself to just being, it
reflects upon itself: it exists. And so for two years the
concept of surreality revisited itself, dragging with it a
universe of determinations. And in this introspection it
rediscovered the images which presided over its genesis,
like a son might redicover his parents, his body assembled
and ready in all its parts for great mysteries, having
already forgotten the old folk. At its starting point,
Surrealism rediscovered the dream, whence it came. But
now the dream is illuminated by the flash of surrealism
and assumes its meaning. As a result, and for the first time
since the world began, when André Breton writes down

his dreams they retain the characteristics of dreaming in the telling. This is because the man who is gathering them has accustomed his memory to experiences other than the meagre realities of the waking. And Robert Desnos learns to dream without sleeping. He contrives to speak his dreams at will.

Dreams, dreams, dreams, with each step the domain of dreams expands. Dreams, dreams, dreams, at last the blue sun of dreams forces the steel-eyed beasts back to their lairs. Dreams, dreams, dreams on the lips of love, on the numbers of happiness, on the teardrops of carefulness, on the signals of hope, on building sites where a whole nation submits to pickaxes. Dreams, dreams, dreams, nothing but dreams where the wind wanders and barking dogs are out on the roads.

Oh magnificent Dream, in the pale morning of buildings, leaning on your elbows on chalk cornices, merging your pure, mobile features with the miraculous immobility of statues, don't ever leave, enticed by dawn's deliberate lies. Clear away this unbearable clearness, this bleeding from the sky which has splashed in my eyes for too long.

Your slipper is in my hair, smoked-faced genie, dazzling shadow rolled up in my breath. Seize the rest of my life, seize every life, rising tide with spume of flowers. Omens over towers, visions at the bottom of ink pools, in the dust of cafés, migrations of birds along the sidelong trajectories of soothsayers, hearts consulted by bloody fingers, the times unfurl from the draperies, rumours usher in your reign and your cyclone, adorable siren, incomparable clown of the caverns, oh dream with backdrop of coral, colour of waterfalls, scent of the wind!

*

1924: under this number, its dragnet behind, trailing a harvest of moon-bream, under this number adorned with disasters, strange stars in its hair, the contagion of dreaming spreads through city districts and countrysides. From clear fields prodigious examples arise.

Who is that man on the shoreline of myths and the sea where all is snow and silence?

Another man, closed to all, lives in his caravan with an army of servants. Another, who barely opened his eyes on this world, died in front of the police and his father just as the carriage was passing beneath the walls of a prison; and that woman, that woman who wrote on the café wall: 'It is better to wipe glasses than gunshots.' And another, what did he do all that time in China between two dreams which have the sound of sea salt? Another, another: you painted night and it was the night itself. And you, the sky, and it was the entire emerald of destiny.

Another dream, yet another dream: the desert above towns, all the shutters identical and the muffled footsteps of life, one would kill for a great deal less. It is for much less that this one is killing himself: a pipeful of romantic rubbish, the decor just how we like it, and a fine chronometer fashioned of gold on the table. And that tall one over there, isn't he ashamed of his impossible little songs? He never imagined that a life eventually gets itself organised. What good did it do that other man in his little cardboard clinic to lay a cold hand on the feelings of mankind and the innocence of family relationships?

Saint-Pol Roux, Raymond Roussel, Philippe Daudet, Germaine Berton, Saint-John Perse, Pablo Picasso, Georges De Chirico, Pierre Reverdy, Jacques Vaché, Léon-Paul Fargue, Sigmund Freud, your portraits adorn the walls of the dream chamber, you are Presidents of the Republic of dreams.

And now here are the dreamers.

*

There is a surrealist light: at the time of day when towns
burst into flame it is the light that falls on the salmon pink
display of silk stockings; it is the light that blazes in the
Benedictine shops and its pale sister in the pearl of
mineral water depots; it is the light that mutely illuminates the blue travel agent's with trips to the battle fields,
Place Vendôme; it is the light that stays late at Barclays
on the Avenue de l'Opéra, when ties are transformed into
fantoms; it is the beam of flashlights on the murdered and
on love. There is a surrealist light in the eyes of every
woman.

A great chunk of realism has just been demolished on
the Boulevard de la Madeleine and through the gap you
can glimpse a landscape which extends to the works at the
Moulin-Rouge, cité Véron, to the demolitions of the
Parisian fortifications, to the sculpture park in the

Tuileries, to the Gobelins blazing the word "PARDON" in neon through the night, to the vaults of the metro where golden Poulain chocolate horses cavalcade, to diamond mines where smugglers run the risk of avaricious laparotomies, to the sulphur springs where little dogs die.

Georges Limbour, hating the almighty sun, more readily tolerates the dawn of the hereafter. He couldn't be prised from the top of the staircase whence the crowd hurled him in the nights of Mainz because of his loathing for crosses and flags and all the gaudy triumphalism of war. André Masson presides over the release of doves at every crossroad: the beautiful knives he will have seen everywhere are ready to be seized at last. If the houses in Paris are mountains it's because they're reflected in Max Morise's monocle: and didn't he defile the great crucifix in the station at Argent (Cher)?

I have seen Paul Eluard trampled by policemen and drivers on a piano and in shattered lightbulbs, there were 30 of them against this starburst. A little later I saw him in the foothills of Champagne in a land of ophite stones. Then he entered the darkness of earth where moral eclipses are chandeliers at a ball unbounded by the ocean, then he came back, he is looking at you. Delteil? That's the young man Francis Jammes pleaded with in the name of his white hair, that young carnivore who passes his days in the Meudon woods with bloodstained images.

Man Ray, who has tamed the biggest eyes in the world, dreams in his own way with knife rests and salt cellars: he gives the light meaning and that's why it knows how to talk. Suzanne are you blonde or brunette? She changes with the wind and you can believe her when she says: water is man's equal.

Who is that prisoner caught in a giant trap? The gestures that Antonin Artaud makes at a distance echo strangely in my heart. Mathias Lubeck, you don't mean it, you're not really going to re-enlist in the colonial service? He says his greatest shame is not being tattooed. Jacques Baron, on his boat, has just met some beautiful pale women: dear friend, do you remember that evening when I left you near Barbès and there were so many prowlers, you weren't thinking about tropical seas then, you were heading on impulse towards summer.

André Breton, there's a man I can say nothing about: if I close my eyes I see him again at Moret, beside the river

Loing, in all the dust-haze of the tow-path. Philippe Soupault for many years was recognised by his curly hair alone, he used to talk to chair upholsterers and laugh unnervingly near noon.

Denise, Denise: does the café of colours in that little road where we always stop still sing so Marvellously every time you pass, are people still killing themselves in the canal and in rue Longue and everywhere you take your clear shadow and your shining eyes?

Jacques-André Boiffard gently refuses to trim his black sideburns. He wears a velvet cap. Everyone please note: he's looking for a job, but doesn't want work. Magic holds no secrets for Roger Vitrac who is setting up a Theatre of Arson where people die as in a forest. He's also organising a revival of the Cult of Absinthe, whose scorched spoons have all been turned over. Jean Carrive, the youngest known surrealist, is notable most of all for his magnificent sense of rebellion: he is rising on the future with a stockpile of blasphemies. Pierre Picon is expanding his empire into Spain. Francis Gérard, less prudent than everyone else, has just thrown himself into the waters of existence: would you know of a woman for him - extremely beautiful and able to make of this twenty-year-old a fallen man forever?

Simone is from the land of humming-birds, those tiny flashes of music, she looks like the time of lime trees. Beaten up by spectators at the 'Petit Casino', and various cafés in the capital, Robert Desnos has often tried out death as a word: Words, he says, are you myths which match the myrtles of Death?

Earthquakes are where Max Ernst, painter of cataclysms as others of battles, feels most at ease and contented. He finds it strange that the earth isn't constantly quaking.

René Crevel has never noticed that this planet is solidly fixed with help from meridians and latitudes: he is more of a sleepwalker than anyone. Great rages and fierce resolve make Pierre Naville a strange being: I can easily see him destined for some kind of assassination attempt on life itself; I wish I could read palms and find out if he's going to be really unlucky.

Marcel Noll, my dear old Noll: you will not attempt to desert us but whose slave are you, if not of the phantoms at the bottom of your eyes? You see, people are but dust.

Imagine, Charles Baron has left the hotel where you used to drop in on each other. He tells me news of his brother. He still receives the favours of that admirable woman to whom I present my compliments once more.

But the one who can do everything, the one who quite simply ranks among heroes, the man who has never resisted existence, the one who is found at the 'Soleil Levant', the one who defies common sense with every breath he takes, is Benjamin Péret, of the beautiful ties, the kind of great poet they just don't make any more, Benjamin Péret who has a whale on a leash, or maybe a little sparrow.

What a shame Georges Malkine is in Nice today. Since he left I have no idea what is elegant and much of the mystery of this badly-lit town has left for the Côte d'Azur. Maxime Alexandre? He thinks I've forgotten him. One does not forget despair.

The most recent news I've had from Renée Gauthier is not good. This prevents me from speaking about that young woman, torn as she is between some kind of passion and an innocence that nothing could make her lose.

My dear Savinio, leave Rome and come here, pushing that cart with its piles of Niobide corpses. All the people I've listed expect you.

Great things are bound to happen. We've suspended a woman from the ceiling of an empty room and worried men come there every day, bearers of weighty secrets. That's how we got to know Georges Bessière, like a punch in the face.

We're working on a task that's enigmatic even for us, in front of a volume of Fantômas fixed to the wall by forks. Visitors, born in faraway climes or at our own door, are helping us design an extraordinary machine which is for killing what exists so that what does not exist may be complete.

At 15, rue de Grenelle we've opened romantic lodgings for unclassifiable ideas and revolutions in progress. Whatever hope remains in this universe of hopelessness will cast its last delirious glances at our ridiculous street stall: 'It's all about coming up with a new declaration of human rights.'

*

In a novel by Marcel Allain, after a thousand twists of fate and thirst, prolonged perils and mirages, the mysterious Coeur-Rouge finally reaches the legendary tomb at the foot of the Celestial Empire where he hopes to find the power-giving ring; and what does he see on the dusty slab of the desecrated burial place as the birds of night fly away? The well defined impression of a Wood-Milne heel.

It seems certain, my friends, that we're dropping our prey to chase after shadows again, that we plumb the depths of the abyss quite in vain. Through the whole of eternity we search for shadows and silence, but what endures is only this one great failure. Why isn't there a monument in every town: To Phaeton, from a grateful humanity? But what does it matter? He had a taste for vertigo and he fell!

*

If I suddenly consider the course of my life, if I forget the training my mind has had - and that's easy - if I master but a little of the meaning of this life that thwarts me, which evades me, suddenly... what does any of it mean?

Suddenly. I expect nothing from the world, I expect nothing from nothing.

The meaning of life, ah that, well: of what use would such a revelation be to me, and how could I apply that knowledge? To know! The stone in the abyss knows only its acceleration or rather doesn't know it.

The only way to look at Man is as the victim of his mirrors, crying out to himself in the pathetic tones of his own histrionics: What is going to happen? As if he had a choice.

*

Oh raging sea of all futility, I am the cliff you erode. Rise, rise, child of moons, oh tide. I am the one who is worn right through, may the wind carry me away. It's a simple thing, when night is too dense, with her spectres and terrors, to stretch out my hands to the beams flashing from revolving lighthouses far away. If I combine the Marvellous constellations with the mental flash that designed them, it's a simple thing. If I sing very quietly. If I go, if I come. If I think. If I simply open these eyes which have seen nothing.

But among all the tunes that I sometimes hum there's one that still gives me an unrestrained illusion of Spring and meadows, an illusion of true Freedom.

I have sometimes lost that tune and then I find it again. Free, free: when the chain of bright rings flies away through the watered silk of sky, when the ball and chain becomes the servants of ankles, when handcuffs are jewellery. And the hermit carves an inscription on the walls of his cell and this makes the sound of wings on the stone. And he sculpts above the rivet the feathered symbol of all the world's loves.

For he is dreaming, and I am dreaming, swept away, I dream. I am dreaming of a long dream where everyone would be dreaming. I do not know what will come of this new undertaking of dreams. I dream at the edge of the world and the night.

Oh what did you want to say to me, men in the distance, shouting with your hands cupped round your mouths, laughing at the sleeper's gestures?

At the edge of the night and of crime, at the edge of crime and of love. Oh Rivieras of the unreal, your casinos without age limits open their playing rooms to those who wish to lose!

Now is the time, believe me, never to win again.

Who is there?

Ah good:

Let in the infinite

Notes on the accompanying CD

The recordings were made at various locations in London and Sussex during February and March 2010.

Extracts from the English translation edited for performance by Susan de Muth. The texts used in the recordings are reproduced below.

Voice: Alex Walker on all tracks

Musical arrangement and performance:
tracks 1,2,4,5 & 6 Tymon Dogg: tracks 3,7 & 8 Alex Thomas

Extracts Arranged for Performance

1. In the Eyes of Every Woman

Music by Tymon Dogg, words Aragon/de Muth

There is a surrealist light:
at the time of day when towns burst into flame
it is the light that falls
on the salmon pink display of silk stockings;
it is the light that blazes in the Benedictine shops
and its pale sister in the pearl of mineral water depots;
it is the light that mutely illuminates the blue travel agent's
with trips to the battle fields, Place Vendôme;
it is the light that stays late at Barclays on the Avenue de l'Opéra, when
ties are transformed into fantoms;
it is the beam of flashlights on the murdered and on love.
There is a surrealist light in the eyes of every woman.

Denise, Denise:
does the café of colours in that little road where we always stop
still sing so marvellously every time you pass?
Are people still killing themselves in the canal
and in rue Longue
and everywhere you take your clear shadow
and your shining eyes.

Simone
is from the land of humming-birds,
those tiny flashes of music,
she looks like the time of lime trees.
The beam of flashlights on the murdered and on love
when towns burst into flame
a surrealist light in the eyes of every woman.

2. Let in the Infinite
Music by Tymon Dogg. Words Aragon/de Muth

Oh raging sea of all futility, I am the cliff you erode.
Rise, rise, child of moons, oh tide.
I am the one who is worn right through,
may the wind carry me away.

It's a simple thing,
when night is too dense,
with her spectres and terrors,
simple
to stretch out my hands
to the revolving beams of lighthouses
far away.

If I combine the constellations
of the Marvellous
with the mental flash that designed them,
it's a simple thing.

If I sing very quietly.
If I go, if I come.
If I think.
If I simply open these eyes
which have seen nothing.

But among all the tunes that I sometimes hum
there's one that still gives me
an unrestrained illusion of Spring and meadows,
an illusion of true Freedom.
I have sometimes lost that tune
and then I find it again.
And the hermit carves an inscription
on the walls of his cell
and this makes the sound of wings on the stone.
And he sculpts above the rivet
the feathered symbol of all the world's loves.

For he is dreaming,
and I am dreaming,
swept away,
I dream.

I am dreaming of a long dream
where everyone would be dreaming.

I dream at the edge of the world and the night.

Oh what do you say to me,
men in the distance,
shouting
with your hands cupped round your mouths,
laughing at the sleeper's gestures?

At the edge of the night and of crime,
at the edge of crime and of love.

Oh Rivieras of the unreal,
your casinos without age limits
open their playing rooms
to those who wish to lose!

Now is the time,
believe me,
never to win again.

Who is there?
Ah good:
let in the infinite.

3. A Period of Trances
Music Alex Thomas. Words Aragon/de Muth

The surrealists...
Young people intent
on intoxication,
derangement.....

Gave themselves up to vice,
Hurled themselves into it.

René Crevel
met a lady
by the sea
and she took him into
hypnotic trances...
like sleepwalking.

An outbreak of trances
swamped the surrealists.
They live only for
these moments of oblivion,
when they talk with the lights out,
without consciousness,
like drowning men in the open air.

He starts to speak;
amid the beer glasses
and saucers
the whole Ocean collapses with its prophetic din
and vapours decorated with oriflammes.
Coincidences characterize the outpourings of the sleepers.
The era of collective hallucinations is born

4. The Hunters
Music Tymon Dogg. Words Aragon/de Muth

Sometimes, quite suddenly,
I lose the whole thread of my life:
sitting in some corner of the universe,
near a smoky dark café,
polished metal before me,
tall, mild-mannered women
ebbing and flowing around me....

At that time we used to meet in the evenings,
like hunters,
comparing what we'd bagged that day,
the tally of beasts we'd invented,
the fantastic plants,
the images we'd shot down.

Overwhelming hallucinations
hallucinations
more usually produced by
ecstatic religious states
or narcotic drugs.

In our strange inner lands
We delighted in the curve of our own exhaustion,
the derangement which came next...
For then
the
Marvellous would appear.

Images that once existed in the mind
took on physical forms,
became tangible reality.

Hallucinations.
We could no longer control them.
We had become *their* domain,
a setting for them.

In bed,
at the moment of falling asleep,
in the street
with our eyes wide open,
with the full apparatus of dread,
we held out our hands to phantoms.

5. Dreams, Dreams, Dreams
Music Tymon Dogg. Words Aragon/de Muth

Dreams, dreams, dreams,
the steel-eyed beasts forced back to their lairs
by the blue sun of dreams.

Dreams, dreams, dreams
on the lips of love,
on the numbers of happiness,
on the teardrops of carefulness,
on the signals of hope,
on building sites
where a whole nation submits
to the authority of pickaxes.

Dreams, dreams, dreams,
nothing but dreams where the wind wanders
and barking dogs are out on the roads.

Oh magnificent Dream,
in the pale morning of buildings,
leaning on your elbows on chalk cornices,
merging your pure, mobile features
with the miraculous immobility of statues,
don't ever leave again enticed by dawn's
deliberate lies.

Clear away this unbearable clearness,
this bleeding from the sky
which has splashed in my eyes for too long.

Your slipper is in my hair, smoked-faced genie,
dazzling shadow rolled up in my breath.

Seize the rest of my life,
seize every life, rising tide with spume of flowers.

The times unfurl from the draperies,
rumours usher in your reign
and your cyclone, adorable siren,
incomparable clown of the caverns,
oh dream with backdrop of coral,
colour of waterfalls,
scent of the wind!

6. Surreality
Music Tymon Dogg. Words Aragon/de Muth

Clouds disperse on the smallest breath
and the same wind brings them back.
An idea too has its golden fringes.

The sun plays a little with the phantoms.
They can dance without ballet shoes
and that broken chain at their ankles
sets the price of their steps.

Oh phantoms with mutable eyes,
children of the shadows,
wait for me,
wait...

I'm nearly there and you turn away.
Do not go beyond the acacia blossom,
the guard of honour, the tribune,
here I am: and yet....
you turn down other hawthorned byways
with your scarves woven from reflections
How to follow an idea?
To follow an idea?

Its paths are full of farandoles.
Masks appear on balconies.
And over there, another kiss.
The whole of life solicits us as we pass,
offering us violets:
everyone's problems in posies.
everyone's problems in posies.

7. Surrealists & the City
Music Alex Thomas. Words Aragon/de Muth

A great chunk of realism has just been demolished
on the Boulevard de la Madeleine
and through the gap
you can glimpse
a cityscape
extending to the works at the Moulin-Rouge,
cité Véron,
to the demolition of Paris's fortifications,
to the sculpture park in the Tuileries,
to the Gobelins blazing the word "PARDON"
in neon through the night,
to the vaults of the metro
where golden Poulain chocolate horses cavalcade,
to diamond mines
where smugglers
run the risk of avaricious laparotomies,
to the sulphur springs
where little dogs die.......
André Masson
presides over the release of doves
at every crossroad...
If the houses in Paris are mountains
it's because they're reflected
in Max Morise's monocle:
and didn't he defile the great crucifix
in the station at Argent (Cher)?

I have seen Paul Eluard trampled by policemen
and drivers on a piano
and in shattered lightbulbs,
there were 30 of them against this starburst.
Man Ray,
who has tamed the biggest eyes in the world,
dreams in his own way
with knife rests and salt cellars:
he gives the light meaning
and that's why it knows how to talk.

8. 15, Rue de Grenelle
Music Alex Thomas. Words Aragon/de Muth

Great things are bound to happen!
We've suspended a woman
from the ceiling
of an empty room!
and worried men come there
every day
with their weighty secrets.

back-dropped by
a collection of Fantômas
fixed to the wall by forks.

Visitors,
are helping us design
an extraordinary machine
which is for killing what exists
so that what does not exist
may be complete.

At 15, rue de Grenelle
we've opened romantic lodgings
for unclassifiable ideas
and revolutions in progress.

Great things are bound to happen!

INDEX OF NAMES